BY THE WATER

BY SHARYN ROTHSTEIN

DRAMATISTS
PLAY SERVICE
INC.

BY THE WATER
Copyright © 2015, Sharyn Rothstein

All Rights Reserved

CAUTION: Professionals and amateurs are hereby warned that performance of BY THE WATER is subject to payment of a royalty. It is fully protected under the copyright laws of the United States of America, and of all countries covered by the International Copyright Union (including the Dominion of Canada and the rest of the British Commonwealth), and of all countries covered by the Pan-American Copyright Convention, the Universal Copyright Convention, the Berne Convention, and of all countries with which the United States has reciprocal copyright relations. All rights, including without limitation professional/amateur stage rights, motion picture, recitation, lecturing, public reading, radio broadcasting, television, video or sound recording, all other forms of mechanical, electronic and digital reproduction, transmission and distribution, such as CD, DVD, the Internet, private and file-sharing networks, information storage and retrieval systems, photocopying, and the rights of translation into foreign languages are strictly reserved. Particular emphasis is placed upon the matter of readings, permission for which must be secured from the Author's agent in writing.

The English language stock and amateur stage performance rights in the United States, its territories, possessions and Canada for BY THE WATER are controlled exclusively by DRAMATISTS PLAY SERVICE, INC., 440 Park Avenue South, New York, NY 10016. No professional or nonprofessional performance of the Play may be given without obtaining in advance the written permission of DRAMATISTS PLAY SERVICE, INC., and paying the requisite fee.

Inquiries concerning all other rights should be addressed to ICM Partners, 730 Fifth Avenue, New York, NY 10019. Attn: Di Glazer.

SPECIAL NOTE
Anyone receiving permission to produce BY THE WATER is required to give credit to the Author(s) as sole and exclusive Author(s) of the Play on the title page of all programs distributed in connection with performances of the Play and in all instances in which the title of the Play appears, including printed or digital materials for advertising, publicizing or otherwise exploiting the Play and/or a production thereof. Please see your production license for font size and typeface requirements.

Be advised that there may be additional credits required in all programs and promotional material. Such language will be listed under the "Additional Billing" section of production licenses. It is the licensee's responsibility to ensure any and all required billing is included in the requisite places, per the terms of the license.

SPECIAL NOTE ON SONGS AND RECORDINGS
For performances of copyrighted songs, arrangements or recordings mentioned in these Plays, the permission of the copyright owner(s) must be obtained. Other songs, arrangements or recordings may be substituted provided permission from the copyright owner(s) of such songs, arrangements or recordings is obtained; or songs, arrangements or recordings in the public domain may be substituted.

ACKNOWLEDGMENTS

This play and its characters are fiction, but I am deeply grateful to Derek Tabacco, Joseph Tirone, Samantha Langello, and the other Staten Islanders who shared their stories of strength and survival with me.

Special thanks to Emily Shooltz, Jason Eagan, Annie MacRae, Doug Hughes, Diana Glazer, and Marilyn & Alan Rothstein (my lifelong dramaturgs and cheerleaders) for their brilliant insight and support.

And to my husband Jeff, who makes my world — and my plays — funnier.

BY THE WATER was commissioned by the Writer's Room (Manhattan Theatre Club, Ars Nova) and received its world premiere at Manhattan Theatre Club (Lynne Meadow, Artistic Director; Barry Grove, Executive Producer) in association with Ars Nova (Jason Eagan, Artistic Director; Renee Blinkwolt, Managing Director) on November 4, 2014. It was directed by Hal Brooks; the scenic design was by Wilson Chin; the costume design was by Jessica Pabst; the lighting design was by Tyler Micoleau; the original music and sound design was by Ryan Rumery; and the production stage manager was E Sara Barnes. The cast was as follows:

MARTY MURPHY .... Vyto Ruginis
MARY MURPHY .... Deirdre O'Connell
SAL MURPHY .... Quincy Dunn-Baker
BRIAN MURPHY .... Tom Pelphrey
PHILIP CARTER .... Ethan Phillips
ANDREA CARTER .... Charlotte Maier
EMILY MANCINI .... Cassie Beck

CHARACTERS

MARTY MURPHY, 62, blue-collar, a community man with a fierce sense of loyalty and of the way the world should work. Tough but charming. Capable of changing moods on a dime.

MARY MURPHY, 60, a woman of faith, sweet but never saccharine. A loving mother and very devoted wife, who has made a life out of looking past the faults of those she loves.

SAL MURPHY, 34, ambitious, smart, a born-again Manhattanite. An innate sense of humor and warmth have been chipped away at by an unforgiving family, but they're still there.

BRIAN MURPHY, 30, a recovering user and all-around badass. Inherited his father's charm and quick laugh; until a recent stint in prison, he lived a dangerously charmed life of being rewarded for the wrong things.

PHILIP CARTER, early 60s, a retired auto-mechanic/body-shop owner, a friendly man with an easy sense of humor, a natural peacekeeper.

ANDREA CARTER, early 60s, funny, shrewd, and opinionated; the kind of great friend and strong woman who quickly becomes more sister than friend.

EMILY MANCINI, 30, Brian's former high school sweetheart; now a wry, self-aware woman coming to terms with a crumbling marriage and the fact that life at 30 doesn't look like what she thought it would. Works in the city, probably lives in Brooklyn or Queens.

PLACE & TIME

The storm-ravaged home of Marty and Mary Murphy, on the eastern coast of Staten Island, New York. After Hurricane Sandy.

NOTE

Slashes (/) indicate where the next line overlaps.

It's helpful if the audience feels like some time has passed between Scenes 10 and 11. Directors and designers are encouraged to find creative ways to express the time-pass.

BY THE WATER

Scene 1

The stage is the ravaged remains of a house. The house is the home of Marty Murphy and his wife, Mary.

When the hurricane hit, the Murphys had lived in this house for 34 years, and before that it belonged to Marty's father. Now: a destroyed couch, crushed end tables, glass everywhere. A four-foot-high watermark. And that smell. Still, they're better off than many. The house, seven short blocks from the water and built up a few feet after the 1992 Nor'easter, is still standing.

It might take us a moment to realize we can see inside of it because there's a huge hole in the living room wall. A moment. Then, voices from the kitchen.

MARY. *(Offstage.)* The smell ...
MARTY. *(Offstage.)* I told you we shoulda brought nose plugs.
MARY. All this food ... What a waste. What a terrible waste. *(Marty enters the living room, bundled for the cold, wearing a surgical mask. He takes it off when he enters the room. The scope of the loss hits him hard. Marty looks like he might be sick, or he might cry. Both. He's a strong man, but this ... Mary enters, holding a blender. She takes off her mask.)* I found the Magic Bullet.
MARTY. Well that's a relief. *(She smiles. He pulls her close. Together, they take in the mess.)* That hole in the wall's gonna make it hard to be intimate.
MARY. The neighbors could use a good show right about now. *(Marty laughs.)* If we still have any. Neighbors.

MARTY. They'll come back. Everybody'll come back. *(Mary nods. She holds up the blender.)*
MARY. You want a smoothie? *(They put their masks back on and stare out, toward the missing wall, toward the sea ...)*

Scene 2

It's still a mess, but they've done what they can: You can see the floorboards. The couch has been moved out. They've moved a lot of debris into piles. The walls are down to their studs.

Lights on Sal Murphy as he enters the house through the tarp-covered missing wall. He's wearing plastic gloves, an industrial-looking parka, sturdy boots.

SAL. Mom? Dad? ... *(Overwhelmed at the destruction.)* Oh my god.
MARY. *(Offstage.)* Is that Sal? *(Enters from the kitchen, her phone to her ear.)* You want something? Diet Pepsi?
SAL. *(Stricken.)* Diet Pepsi? *(Marty enters with contractor bags, which he begins filling with debris.)*
MARTY. Nice outfit. You're going fly-fishing?
SAL. Mom said you needed help clearing stuff out. *(Marty shoots Mary a look.)*
MARY. Your back.
MARTY. My back's fine.
SAL. And I couldn't find my HazMat suit, so —
MARY. Your what suit? *(To Marty.)* His what suit?
SAL. HazMat, like those big, with the — nevermind. This is ... *(Marty throws Sal a bag, but Sal doesn't even know where to start.)*
MARTY. It looks worse than it is. *(Slight beat.)* Well no, it looks just as bad as it is.
MARY. *(Into the phone.)* Hello? Hello?
MARTY. She's been on hold all / week.
MARY. *(To Sal.)* / Insurance. *(Into the phone.)* Are you there? *(Exits for the driveway.)*
SAL. Everything's ...

MARTY. And we're the lucky ones. You heard about Kathy Dolan? *(Shakes his head.)* She was a nice woman.
SAL. A nice woman who should've evacuated.
MARTY. *(Fierce.)* Watch yourself, smartass. *(A tense moment quickly interrupted by Mary, phone still to her ear, who enters with a suitcase or two.)*
MARY. *(Indicating the phone.)* At least I like the music they play. That'd be an interesting job, don't you think? Picking out the music for when people are on hold? Maybe not. *(Starts unpacking the suitcase. Sal watches her, astonished.)*
SAL. *What are you* — ? I thought you were just cleaning it out ... you didn't tell me you were *moving back*. *(Mary unpacks a small cross and hangs it on the wall.)*
MARY. It's not exactly front page news: "Married couple moves home."
SAL. You're staying here. *(Mary finds a framed photo or embroidered saying in the suitcase. She finds a place for it.)*
MARTY. Where else should we stay?
SAL. At the hotel.
MARTY. Your mother hated that hotel. And it wasn't cheap.
MARY. It wasn't cheap. And do you know the maid stole my socks?
SAL. Mom, the maid didn't steal your socks.
MARY. Then who stole them?
SAL. No one stole your socks. Why would the maid — ?
MARY. Why wouldn't she? I have nice socks.
MARTY. *(Suggestive, playful.)* You should see your mother's socks.
SAL. Dad. Ugh.
MARY. Here we are, *refugees*, and they're stealing from us. I'm never going back there. In fact, I'm never going to another hotel as long as I live.
SAL. Because you were such a world-traveler before. The whole hospitality industry just shuddered.
MARY. *(Serious.)* It's not a home, Sally. A woman like me needs a home.
SAL. Mom. Look around. *(Then, gentle.)* Why don't you at least move in with me, for a while?
MARTY. *(Laughs.)* To your million-dollar-a-month water closet in the city?
SAL. It's not a million / dollars —
MARY. / We'd stick out the windows.
SAL. At least there are windows. And heat.

MARTY. The generator's up, and I got some space heaters. We're fine, if we huddle. The insurance money's gonna kick in soon, then I can start the big work. Till then I got the top tarp Home Depot sells.
MARY. You got the top tarp?
MARTY. Tippy top.
MARY. Tell you the truth, that tarp's the tops.
SAL. What about the mold? Pollution? The toxins, whatever it is?
MARY. Your father called in a favor. Mo the Mold Guy. I don't think that's his real name.
MARTY. Didn't you see the sign on the door? We're allowed back in. To our own home, we're allowed back in. *(Indicating the open wall.)* Besides, we're well-ventilated. *(Sal groans in frustration. Marty puts his hand on Sal's shoulder.)* Sally. I think it was my great, wise Uncle Redmond who once told me: Nobody knows what's coming down the pike. Just when you think you've got it all figured out, you let out a fart that turns out to be a crap.
SAL. That's lovely, Dad. Thank you for that.
MARY. We gotta have faith, Sal. That's all we've got. Where's Jennifer?
SAL. At work.
MARY. It's a Saturday. Isn't it a Saturday?
SAL. Weekends are really busy for her.
MARY. We haven't seen her in a while. I thought, because of the storm ...
SAL. She wanted to come. / She's working.
MARY. *(Shaking her head.)* / I just don't know how you're going to have children.
SAL. Mom.
MARY. She's always working.
SAL. *Mom.* Would you stop changing the — ?
MARY. *(Into the phone.)* Hello?

MARTY.	MARY.
You know my father built this house with his own two hands.	Yes, I'm Mary Murphy, I've been — Let me give you my —

SAL. No, he didn't. Grandpa bought this house from a developer.
MARY. *(Into the phone. Sigh.)* Yes, I'll hold.
MARTY. But he built the back deck. I know 'cause I did most of the heavy lifting.
SAL. Weren't you like 10?
MARTY. You shoulda seen me at 10. Like an ox, I was.

MARY. If you mean stubborn as all get-out. Some things never change. *(Marty charges at her like an ox. She swats him away playfully.)*
MARTY. And the garage. We built the garage too.
SAL. You hired someone to build the garage. I remember.
MARTY. So? Do you say the Egyptians built the pyramids or do you say the Egyptians hired someone to build the pyramids?
SAL. They didn't hire someone, they enslaved them.
MARTY. Details. Always details with / you.
MARY. / Are you staying for dinner? I'll make more.
SAL. You're eating here?! Where are you keeping the food?
MARTY. Somehow the fridge survived the storm.
MARY. She was always a good fridge.
MARTY. A survivor, that fridge.
MARY. We oughta take her picture, put it in the paper.
SAL. There's definitely pollution here. Something in the air. You two are acting like you're on drugs.
MARTY. *(Puts his arm around his wife.)* There's nothing like a little near-fatal disaster to remind you how lucky you are to have the people you love.
SAL. You *are* lucky. Incredibly lucky. How many times can you be so lucky?
MARY. As many times as Christ allows.
SAL. *Mom. This is the second hurricane in two years.* You stay here, you'll have another one just like it to deal with.
MARY. You don't know that.
SAL. Yes I do! You shouldn't be living here, five, six feet above sea level —
MARTY. There's storms everywhere. What happens if you live in California? You go out to get the paper, your front yard splits in two.
SAL. I don't want to have to worry every time there's a bad weather report!
MARTY. So don't worry! You always worried too much. Brian never worried a day in his life.
SAL. And that worked out great for him, didn't it? *(Marty glares at Sal. Mary immediately defuses.)*
MARY. He's doing really good now. That's all that matters. *(To Sal.)* Which you'd know, if you'd seen / him —
MARTY. That's right. / He's a chef. In Manhattan!
SAL. At an Olive Garden.
MARTY. So what it's an Olive Garden? It's still in Manhattan.

SAL. Which is embarrassing in and of itself.
MARTY. He was always the uppity one. That's the real reason you want us to move. This neighborhood was never good enough for you. "Staten Island." You always said it with a nose-wrinkle. Like it tasted wrong.
SAL. There's nothing wrong with Staten Island.
MARY. Then why didn't you move here?
SAL. It's not for me.
MARTY. Exactly.
MARY. You could've saved a lot of money. Had a whole house instead of a one-bedroom.
SAL. One-and-a-half-bedroom.
MARY. I'll never understand that. What's half a bedroom?
SAL. It's a bedroom without a window. That you can't fit a bed in. *(Mary and Marty exchange a look.)* Look, I'm not telling you to leave the Island. I'm just asking you to move farther in. Away from the water.
MARTY. *(Pulls his wife close.)* This is where we belong, Sal. This is where everyone knows us: We're Marty and Mary Murphy. We have history here. Besides, we've survived storms like this before.
SAL. Not like *this*.
MARTY. We've survived plenty.
SAL. *(To Mary.)* So you're not afraid? Staying here. You're not afraid? *(Beat. Mary can't answer. It might take Marty by surprise, but he recovers quickly.)*
MARTY. Of course she's afraid right now. Look at what we've been through. But it'll fade. Three months, four months from now. The sun comes out. It'll go away.
SAL. *(An appeal.)* Mom …
MARY. *(Looks at him, maybe swallowing something back. Maybe warning him.)* Let it go, Sally.
SAL. Mom.
MARY. *(Tough.)* Let it go. *(In the kitchen, Brian enters.)*
BRIAN. Mom, Dad? *(He enters the room. Hugs, kisses.)*
MARY. Brian! What a / surprise!
MARTY. *(Very pleased.)* / Bri! *(Brian sees Sal. It's the first time in a very long time.)*
BRIAN. *(To Marty.)* Thought you could use an extra set of hands.
MARTY. I could. My back's been killing me. *(Sal looks at his father, incredulous.)*
BRIAN. *(Takes in the disaster.)* Whoa. *(Beat.)* What's for dinner?

Scene 3

Later that night. Sal sits at a plastic folding table on a folding chair, a six-pack of beer in front of him, drinking. Brian enters from upstairs.

This is the first time they've seen each other in nearly three years, and it shows in the little awkward tensions that keep creeping in. Still, they're trying.

BRIAN. You gonna try to make the ferry?
SAL. I don't know. I don't like the idea of them being alone. If something happens, nobody's around ...
BRIAN. So you're gonna stay over? In this? What if your polo gets wrinkled?
SAL. Very funny.
BRIAN. You might get some dirt on your khakis —
SAL. Hilarious. *(Indicating upstairs.)* How's the shrine?
BRIAN. Gonna have to throw out the stuff on the walls.
SAL. *(Ribbing.)* The Mötley Crüe poster's finally coming down?
BRIAN. *(Right back at him.)* Guess so. What'd you do with your Dave Matthews one?
SAL. I never had a Dave Matthews poster. The concert shirt ... *(Brian smirks. A genuinely warm moment between them, followed quickly by an uncomfortable silence.)* Thanks for the beers.
BRIAN. Figured you'd need 'em. I'd make us something to eat too, if the kitchen wasn't a toxic-waste site, and the oven was working.
SAL. They said when they opened it a pair of old boots came out.
BRIAN. Nah, that was probably just Mom's pot roast.
SAL. *(Laughs.)* Dad loves her cooking.
BRIAN. Dad loves everything about her.
SAL. What's not to love? When has she ever not done exactly what he wants her to do?
BRIAN. How's Jenn?
SAL. She's okay. Trying to start her own firm, so she's working a lot.
BRIAN. PR.

SAL. Right.
BRIAN. *(Funny voice.)* Public relations.
SAL. *(With a smile.)* Yeah.
BRIAN. She didn't want to come out?
SAL. She did, but you know ...
BRIAN. Baby pressure.
SAL. ... yeah.
BRIAN. Sorry about Christmas. It was nice of her, you, to invite me. I just, they were offering time and a half ...
SAL. You didn't miss anything. According to Dad, it didn't even count 'cause Jenn made turkey instead of ham and we had a fake tree. "You think you put a star on a toilet brush it's a Christmas tree?"
BRIAN. *(Laughs.)* Everything's always gotta be his way. *(Sal nods. Slight beat.)*
SAL. Hey, remember DeFizz?
BRIAN. DeFizz ...
SAL. Marky DeFizzio. The kid with the unibrow. / DeFuzzio.
BRIAN. / DeFuzzio! Right.
SAL. He's got a real estate office now, on Richmond.
BRIAN. Yeah? He got a job with that eyebrow?
SAL. *(Making a unibrow with his fingers.)* He's got his face on all these posters in front / of people's houses —
BRIAN. *(Laughing.)* / No way.
SAL. I called him up. He said he'd be happy to show them some places. I know they're both stubborn as hell but maybe if they see something they like ... We just gotta get them to Marky's office.
BRIAN. That's an idea.
SAL. It's a *good* idea.
BRIAN. Sure.
SAL. There's no way Dad'll listen to me alone, but I thought if we both tell 'em, together ... *(An entreaty. Brian looks away.)*
BRIAN. Look, I just got out. 29 months for being a fuck-up. That's actually what the judge called me. What did Mom ever do to deserve a delinquent like me? And Dad —
SAL. *("Give me a break.")* Dad.
BRIAN. No, really. Before he fucked it all up with the IRS, Dad was on every community board ever invented. Always raising money for charity. He was like the Bono of Staten Island. They're good people and I gave them nothing but grief. How can I ask them to leave? What right do I have? *(Beat. Sal shakes his head.)*

SAL. I shoulda known.
BRIAN. What's that mean?
SAL. Why would you help?
BRIAN. I'm trying to explain to you —
SAL. Bullshit. You're trying to sound big, or noble, or some shit like that. Make it about them and their happiness. That's not what it's about.
BRIAN. Oh yeah, what's it about / Sal?
SAL. / It's about the simple fact that you are constitutionally unable to put anyone else's needs before your own.
BRIAN. That's so.
SAL. And it always has been.
BRIAN. And you're so good at it.
SAL. I try to be / yeah —
BRIAN. / Yeah you got a fucking master's degree in putting other people first.
SAL. I'm not getting into this with you —
BRIAN. What about your wife? You put her first?
SAL. Every day.
BRIAN. Maybe that's the problem.
SAL. There is no problem.
BRIAN. You're miserable. You don't think that's a problem?
SAL. Who said I'm miserable?
BRIAN. Your face said it. Your fucking shoulders say it.
SAL. I've been under a lot of stress, at work.
BRIAN. You sell internet ads.
SAL. I *manage* people who sell internet ads. And don't start with me — you're a short-order cook at Olive Garden.
BRIAN. And I *like* it. So you can stop acting like all I do is throw slop on a plate and add a little parsley. Because it's cooking. It's actual cooking, it's fucking hard work and I like it. And by the way, *some of us*, we don't have that many options.
SAL. Yeah, and why is that?
BRIAN. You oughta know. *(Beat.)*
SAL. Forget it. I shouldn'ta even called. Shoulda let you come out on your own, 9, 10 months from now when everything was already / done.
BRIAN. / I was gonna come out on my own.
SAL. Sure.
BRIAN. I *was*.

SAL. *When? (A cold beat.)*
BRIAN. You think I want Mom and Dad living like this, *in* this, right now? What son would want that? But it's not going to stay like this. Dad's gonna fix it up. People will come back.
SAL. You're just as crazy as they are. Open your eyes! Nobody's coming back to this.
BRIAN. Yeah they will. You know why? 'Cause starting over from scratch, some place you don't know, with people who don't give a shit about you? It sucks. It's exhausting. And it's lonely. It's really, really lonely. *(Beat.)* So I'm sorry, but you want them to move, you gotta do it on your own. *(Gets up. Grabs the beers.)* And I'm taking the beers.
SAL. You're not supposed to drink!
BRIAN. Then I guess I'll just look at them. *(Exits. Sal sits alone.)*

Scene 4

Mary sits with Andrea Carter, a longtime friend and neighbor, on plastic chairs. Andrea's husband, Philip, looks through the debris.

ANDREA. It's all gone. Every picture I ever took.
MARY. Oh gosh.
PHILIP. And you know she took a lot of them.
MARY. I know. *(Laughs.)*
PHILIP. Couldn't blow your nose in our house without my wife taking a picture.
ANDREA. He's exaggerating. All those memories …
PHILIP. You still have the memories.
MARY. You'll always have the memories.
ANDREA. Not if I get Alzheimer's.
MARY. That's true.
PHILIP. Don't encourage her. She's sure she's going to get Alzheimer's.
ANDREA. It runs in my family.
PHILIP. It runs in everyone's family. You live to a certain age, you get Alzheimer's.
ANDREA. The point is, it's very likely I'll get it. And what then?

You'll put me in the home and the people in the home — if they're good people, if they're not abusive —
PHILIP. What kind of home do you think I'm putting you in?
ANDREA. They're expensive, you might have to compromise.
PHILIP. That's true.
ANDREA. — the people in the home will say to me, Andrea, poor thing, why don't we look at pictures of your family together? But there won't be any. And I won't even know that there *used* to be pictures to tell them. So they'll think, what kind of woman is this? She never took a picture of her family.
MARY. I'll come. I'll tell them what happened.
ANDREA. Sure. Unless you've got Alzheimer's too.
PHILIP. Enough with the Alzheimer's! *(Sal enters from upstairs. Hugs, kisses.)*
SAL. Hey Phil. / Andrea.
ANDREA. / Sally!
PHILIP. Sal, I didn't know you still knew how to get out here.
SAL. Very / funny.
PHILIP. / You know the ferry's free now, you don't gotta pay.
SAL. *(Hamming it up.)* Free? The guy out front told me it was twenty bucks. *(Phil laughs.)*
ANDREA. Don't listen to him. You look good.
MARY. Doesn't he? So handsome. Just imagine that face on a baby.
SAL. Mom ...
ANDREA. And you're still married?
SAL. Yeah, of course.
ANDREA. You never know these days. All three of our girls got divorced.
MARY. It wasn't meant to be.
ANDREA. Sure, but what does that say about us?
PHILIP. That we're shmucks for paying for three weddings.
ANDREA. You know, Sal, Emily's on her way in. She's coming over to see the disaster for herself. You two could get together.
SAL. Thanks Andrea. I'll call her.
ANDREA. You need her number?
PHILIP. Uh oh, here we go ...
SAL. I can send her an email.
ANDREA. You have her email?
MARY. *(Under her breath.)* Andrea ...
SAL. I'm sure she's on Facebook.

ANDREA. *(Writing down the number.)* Let me give you her number. I know she'd like to see you. She's been very lonely. *(Sal and Mary exchange a look.)*

MARY. Andrea, he's *married*.

ANDREA. Things change. *(Marty enters lugging a bag of hardware. Hugs, kisses.)*

MARTY. / Hey look who the cat dragged in!

ANDREA. / Marty. It's good to see you. It's good to see anyone.

PHILIP. *(To Marty.)* Thanks for calling about the house. You must've been the first person back here.

MARTY. Couldn't sleep not knowing.

MARY. He was going door-to-door, making sure everybody was out … I couldn't bear even thinking about it.

SAL. *(To Phil.)* How *is* your house?

PHILIP. What house?

SAL. No. / Really?

ANDREA. / He's exaggerating. It's still there, just a shell. We had water right up to the ceiling.

MARY. Oh gosh.

ANDREA. And the roof. We're missing half of it.

MARY. Gosh / gosh gosh.

SAL. / I'm sorry to hear that.

PHILIP. *(With a shrug.)* I always wanted a skylight.

SAL. So you're staying too.

MARTY. Of course they are. *(Andrea and Philip look at each other. A beat the others notice.)*

MARY. Of course you are. *(Another look between Phil and Andrea. They haven't been looking forward to this.)*

PHILIP. Truth is, it's been nice staying in Montclair, with Joy and the kids.

ANDREA. It's been nice. Every morning, a hug from Max, a hug from Sophie.

MARY. Nice, sure, but this is your home.

ANDREA. It *was* our home. It'd be a big cost, to rebuild.

PHILIP. You never know how much they're gonna cover. Not to mention the premiums now …

MARTY. *(Conceding just a bit.)* The premiums are gonna be something, but / c'mon …

MARY. Andrea. We need you here! You lost all your things. It's terrible.

But think of the people you would lose if you moved away. People are harder to replace than things.
ANDREA. It would be incredibly hard. But look, it's already hard. A lifetime of pictures … *(Beat.)*
PHILIP. *(To Marty, gingerly.)* You haven't thought about it? Moving?
SAL. Unbelievably no, they haven't.
MARY. Don't be smart. Of course we've thought about it.
MARTY. Of course we've *thought* about it. *(To Sal.)* Why are you still here? *(To Mary.)* Why's he still here? Don't you have to work?
MARY. Marty —
SAL. I can work from my phone. They know the situation.
PHILIP. *(To Marty.)* So I guess you're not going to the meeting.
SAL. What meeting?
MARTY. *(Waving it off.)* It's a pipe dream, Phil.
ANDREA. *(To Mary.)* You're not going to the meeting?
MARY. *(Uneasy, to Andrea.)* We just got so much to do / around here …
SAL. / What're you talking about?
PHILIP. / People are tired of fighting back nature, Marty.
MARTY. It's a trade-off. You wanna live by the water, it's a trade-off —
ANDREA. Some trade-off!
MARY. I find it hard to believe they're just gonna give out checks —
MARTY. 'Cause you're smart. Smarter than all these fools ready to hand everything off to the politicians.
SAL. *What meeting?*
PHILIP. Rudy Tosetti, Father Driscoll, they're organizing a meeting to see who's interested in a buy-out.
SAL. A buy-out?
ANDREA. From the government. Buy all the houses in the neighborhood and knock 'em all down before the next storm can do it.
MARY. *(A sad echo.)* Knock 'em all down.
PHILIP. Oakwood Beach, they had a meeting a month ago already —
SAL. And you're eligible, you think this area's eligible —
PHILIP. We could be. If enough people want it.
SAL. *(To Marty.)* Were you gonna tell me about this?
MARTY. Why would we tell *you*? It's a scam / anyway.
PHILIP. / A scam? Marty …
SAL. Jesus Dad. Why couldn't it be a good thing, just this once? The government wants to help so the next time it floods the taxpayers won't have to bail you out?

19

MARTY. Don't you use that language around me.
SAL. "Taxpayers"?
MARY. *(Warning.)* Sal.
MARTY. *Bail out.* The government isn't bailing us out. We're hard-working people. We deserve to keep our homes. You actually think they're gonna come in here, mow everything down, and give it over to the birds and bees? Beautiful waterfront property? They're gonna pay us to get lost, then sell it to some big-deal millionaires.
ANDREA. Marty, you have to admit. It'd be a good thing for a lot of people.
PHILIP. A lot of / people.
ANDREA. / Donna and Lionel? Jim and Camille? They got nothing standing. If the state's willing to give them some money —
MARTY. Sure. Of course. I hope the state gives us *all* money. So we can rebuild.
ANDREA. Rebuild why? So it can be destroyed all over again? What's the point?
MARTY. The point? This is our home. That's the point! I never woulda thought you two of all people would give up on this place.
PHILIP. That's not fair, Marty.
ANDREA. *(Getting worked up.)* You think we gave up? You think, what, we *chose* for this to happen to us? To everything we love?
MARTY. When the going gets tough —
ANDREA. "Tough"? You think this is "tough"? You can still live in your home! You've got your damned fridge! What do we have? We have NOTHING.
MARY. Andrea —
ANDREA. We have NOTHING. Not one dish towel. Not one spoon. There is *NOTHING LEFT. Look at me.* I am 60 years old. And I HAVE NOTHING. *(She dissolves into tears.)*
MARTY. I'm sorry.
MARY. Shhh. You know he didn't mean it that way …
ANDREA. Why should I stay here and be reminded, every day, every second, of all this … this waste …
MARY. Because it'll get better. It has to get better.
ANDREA. You're right. Somewhere else. Somewhere else it'll be better. *(Sniffs, wipes her eyes.)* Let's go, Phil. Emily's probably waiting for us.
MARY. Please don't leave upset.
ANDREA. How could I not be upset? Look around you. How could any of us not be upset? *(Takes her bag and leaves.)*

MARTY. Phil, I didn't mean …
PHILIP. It's not easy for us, y'know. There's nothing easy about it.
MARY. Of course not.
PHILIP. We thought we left Mr. Figgy behind. We'd been in such a rush to leave, shoving things into bags … I had the dog case, but no dog. *(To Marty.)* You know how I feel about that ankle-biting yapper. Always pissing all over everything. *(To Sal.)* When I was a kid I had a black lab, big beautiful dog. Now? I've got a sewer rat in a cardigan. Even so, we're sitting at Joy's, watching the storm come in on the TV, and I felt just as shitty as a man can feel. It was like every news reporter was saying, "Look at this, this violence, this destruction. Nothing can survive this. And YOU, you left your dog here!" *(He shakes his head.)* Then, maybe an hour into it, Max says, "Grandpa, didn't your suitcase used to be by the door?" Now it's halfway across the kitchen, and it's "yap yap yap!" *(He laughs.)* We were in such a rush, I must've thrown him in there and forgotten about it. But for that hour … And that was just my dog you know? That was just my dog. And I don't even like him. *(Beat.)* I like to think of myself as a strong man … but some things you just can't live through twice. *(He leaves. Silence.)*
MARY. I can't believe it. I just can't …
SAL. People move, Mom. It's something people do.
MARTY. It's something you people do.
SAL. Who's "you people"?
MARTY. Your generation. You people who only care about your jobs, about climbing higher and higher. Who have no connections, no responsibilities —
SAL. Just because I don't go to church —
MARTY. Don't go to church. Don't even know where the nearest church is!
SAL. Y'know what I believe in? *Science.* You replace "faith" with "fact" and suddenly everything makes a lot more sense —
MARY. You can't replace faith, Sally. It doesn't work that way.
MARTY. Your mother and I, we have a *community*. You don't get a community handed to you. You work for it.
SAL. This is rich, this *civics* lesson / coming from you.
MARTY. / You're welcoming to your neighbors. You participate in events. You know people and they know you. Those relationships make you human.
SAL. You think I'm not human?

MARY. Of course he thinks you're / human —
MARTY. / You're a robot. A cash / register.
MARY. / He's not a robot!
SAL. Would a cash register care if you stayed here and got washed away in the next storm?
MARY. Don't talk / like that.
SAL. / Would a cash register be here helping / you?
MARTY. / Helping what? I've been pulling out floorboards all morning. Where were you helping?
SAL. I had a late start. I'll help this afternoon.
MARTY. What is this, vacation? You think this is a time share?
MARY. Some timeshare! SAL. Yeah I think it's a timeshare.
MARTY. I'm just saying, he's so set on us leaving, but meanwhile, it's been three days, and he's still sitting here. Can someone explain that to me? Don't you have a wife to go home to?
MARY. Marty!
SAL. Don't make this about me. You're upset because your friends are leaving. Because after what they went through they can't bear to stay. It's not my fault.
MARTY. I want you out of the house.
MARY. Everyone needs to calm / down —
MARTY. / You're bad juju. I'm trying to fix things, make it right, and you're here, all negativity and crap attitude and I want you out.
SAL. No problem. Should I go through the door or the wall?
MARTY. Go through the floor for all I care, just GO.
MARY. Marty! GET A GRIP! *(Pissed, Sal heads out.)* What's wrong with you?
MARTY. This is my house. My town. And he's telling me to leave? He doesn't know the first thing about building a life. Not the FIRST THING.
MARY. You're getting worked up. *(Then, gingerly.)* Maybe it's not such a bad thing, a buy-out —
MARTY. That's what you want?
MARY. No. I don't know.
MARTY. Sweetheart, we discussed this. There's no way they'll get the full value.
MARY. I know.
MARTY. You think the government's really gonna —
MARY. I know, I know.

MARTY. Even half of it. We'd barely have enough to get a place worth living in.
MARY. We'd make do.
MARTY. Honey, a rental? A tiny place? And where? Off Hylan Boulevard, with the noise and the garbage? After all these years on a peaceful street? Is that what we worked for our whole lives?
MARY. It'd be hard.
MARTY. You'd be miserable. And I couldn't live with that, seeing you *make do*. *(Beat.)* There's a lot of work here. It's not gonna be easy. But we know what our life here looks like. We know how good it can be. I was a kid here. We started our family here. How many mornings have we had, walking down to the beach, the sun coming up, looking out over Brooklyn, thinking "Brooklyn. What schmucks." I've been the luckiest man on the planet.
MARY. And you think it's all 'cause we lived here?
MARTY. Not because we lived here. Because we made here our home. Sal doesn't have a home. He's got a square box with a sheet of glass and a bunch of guys in the lobby who call him "mister." If it washed away tomorrow, he'd find another one, just like it. It's interchangeable. Is that how life should be?
MARY. No. It's not. *(Marty starts to put on his coat.)* Where are you going?
MARTY. The government wants to come in here and bribe people away with money? Not while I'm around.
MARY. Marty, you can't make people's decisions for them.
MARTY. But you can show them why they're wrong. You can show them why it's worth staying.
MARY. What do you got that's a better argument than what the storm showed them?
MARTY. You're not on my side?
MARY. I'm always on your side. I was born on your side. But we've got enough to do in our own home. You can't fix the whole town, you can't make it right for everyone, as much as I know you want to.
MARTY. But I can try. Because it's worth it. It's worth it. *(He exits. Mary is alone, unsure.)*

Scene 5

Emily, bundled in a big floppy hat and her father's winter coat, and Brian sit on a pile of debris overlooking the ravaged beach.

EMILY. What a mess.
BRIAN. Yeah. *(Emily laughs.)* What?
EMILY. Nothing. Just, I was thinking this is like, the physical embodiment of my marriage. Like if my marriage looked like something, this would be it.
BRIAN. You're better off.
EMILY. You think so?
BRIAN. He was kind of a prick.
EMILY. Yeah.
BRIAN. The first time I met him, at that party at your sister's place, I was like, "Hey Dan, pass me a beer." And he was like, "It's *Daniel.*"
EMILY. *(Very familiar with it.)* Yeah.
BRIAN. None of us understood why you were marrying him.
EMILY. Wow. Thanks for speaking up before the fact.
BRIAN. Would you have wanted me to?
EMILY. I wouldn't have listened anyway. I thought he was my ticket out. The last train coming. I should've taken a bus. *(Brian laughs.)* I'm glad I ran into you. I was surprised.
BRIAN. They need help.
EMILY. I can't believe they're staying. I can't believe anyone would stay.
BRIAN. It's a nice place. I always took it for granted. But once you leave, you kinda see it different. *(Emily nods.)*
EMILY. How about you? Any prospects?
BRIAN. Prospects?
EMILY. Women. Anyone you've been seeing?
BRIAN. No, not really.
EMILY. Really? You look good. And I woulda thought, after where you been…?
BRIAN. Well you know. Some girls here and there. But nothing …
EMILY. You better be telling me the truth. It's no fair leading a girl on, not when her life looks like this beach.

BRIAN. You still think about me?
EMILY. I was going to visit you, but I could never decide what shoes to wear. Heels felt too ... oh-la-la. Sneakers just seemed too casual ... Too, "Just dropping in on an old friend for *visiting hours.* Happens every day."
BRIAN. An old friend?
EMILY. You know what I mean.
BRIAN. I thought about you too.
EMILY. Yeah?
BRIAN. We were young, huh?
EMILY. And stupid.
BRIAN. And this beach.
EMILY. We defiled this beach.
BRIAN. *(Big smile.)* Yeah we did.
EMILY. It was a great place to be a young, stupid teenager. *(Slight beat.)* You still see her, when you look at me? You still see that girl in a push-up bra with nothing to push up, with her big hair and her newly straightened teeth?
BRIAN. I still see her.
EMILY. *(Smiles tightly.)* Tell her I say hi. *(Beat.)* The whole town's picking up. It's like our entire childhood's just gonna be ... washed away. My parents are moving to Montclair. So there won't be any reason to come back here. I won't see you again. Unless, you know ... *(She is very close to him.)*
BRIAN. I've been seeing someone.
EMILY. Oh. Okay —
BRIAN. I lied to you because ... I guess because that's just what I do.
EMILY. Right.
BRIAN. I'm trying to change that. I am. But ...
EMILY. Old habits.
BRIAN. No. It's because I'm a fuck-up. I'm trying not to be.
EMILY. Well you didn't have to tell me. Or you coulda told me after. So, I guess that's ... an improvement or something.
BRIAN. Yeah. *(Beat.)* We could still ...
EMILY. *(Laughs, bitter.)* Yeah, I'm used to being treated like crap, so why not do it some more?
BRIAN. I didn't mean —
EMILY. They're leaving. My parents. It's for the best. When things are this bad ... you should just leave. *(She stands.)* Sorry I didn't visit you. I guess the sneakers would've been just fine. *(She leaves.)*

Scene 6

Sal and Mary sit in the waiting area of DeFuzzio's real estate office. Mary is obviously uncomfortable.

MARY. We shouldn't be doing this.
SAL. Mom.
MARY. How does it look, Dad's out there trying to get people to stay, and I'm in here, *looking at houses* —
SAL. You're not doing anything wrong.
MARY. This is what Judas felt like.
SAL. Mom. It's your house too.
MARY. Marriage means compromise Sally. It's a give and take.
SAL. Yeah. You give. He takes.
MARY. You always act like he's never done anything for me. Your father was the first man who ever treated me with respect. You think that's nothing? You think it's nothing to have somebody who holds you up when your parents die? Somebody who tells you jokes when you're in the doctor's office, waiting to hear if what you've got might kill you? I'm not saying I don't do a lot for him. I do a lot for him. But it's a two-way street. You know how important it is to have someone who makes you laugh? Does Jennifer make you laugh? She makes you happy?
SAL. Yeah. *(Genuine.)* Yeah, she makes me happy.
MARY. Things are okay, with you two? It's not that I'm not happy having you here, but four days —
SAL. Things are great.
MARY. Good. *(Beat.)* Of course nothing makes you laugh like children.
SAL. Mom ...
MARY. It's true. I remember when we were potty-training you. We were always saying, "Go Sally! Pee in the potty like a big boy!"
SAL. *(Embarrassed, looking around.)* Mom ...
MARY. Then one time we're at the store, you were three or four, which is late to still be in diapers by the way —
SAL. Thank you ...

MARY. — and Daddy leaves you in the booth so he can go take a leak and you, you were always such a helper, somehow you get yourself on the PA system and you yell out to the whole grocery store: "Attention shoppers: My daddy's gonna pee in the potty like a big boy!" *(Laughs.)* Then you go — "And melons are on sale in aisle two!" *(Laughs again.)* You were so proud of yourself. And I'd never seen him laugh so hard … *(Beat.)* I don't know why some parents and some children don't get along. It was never easy for you and your dad like it was for him and Brian. But that doesn't mean he doesn't love you. If you ask me, it means he loves you more. Because he's had to work for it.
SAL. Wow. I wish I could say that makes me feel better.
MARY. Ask me what the key to life is. Go on, ask me.
SAL. I know what you're gonna say.
MARY. You don't know what I'm gonna say.
SAL. God.
MARY. Chocolate. *(Sal laughs.)* And kindness. Even when it's hard. Especially when it's hard. *(Beat.)* This is a waste of time. How could he show us anything better than what we've got?
SAL. What you *had*. Mom, I know this is hard. But think about what happened when that storm hit.
MARY. Don't.
SAL. If you'd been there —
MARY. I said stop.
SAL. A thirty-foot wave —
MARY. *You don't think I think about that?* You don't think I wake up at night, thinking about that?
SAL. Then *why* — ?
MARY. Because God spared us! Maybe He did it so we could come back and rebuild.
SAL. Mom —
MARY. Don't shake your head at me. We coulda been dead. But we're not. There's a reason for that. *There has to be a reason.*
SAL. *(Gentle.)* Maybe there is a reason. But it's not so you can stay there. *(Beat.)* I know Dad wants you to believe he can rebuild the house so that it never gets hit again, but he can't. It's just not possible. You wouldn't be here if you didn't know, deep down, that's the truth. *(Beat.)*
MARY. I'll only look at places with a washer/dryer.
SAL. He knows that.

MARY. And no stainless steel fridge. I like magnets on a fridge.
SAL. I told him.
MARY. He's not gonna be able to find a place without a stainless steel fridge. It's all anybody wants anymore.
SAL. You can always replace the fridge.
MARY. Replace the fridge. What's the point of moving, if you've gotta replace the fridge?
SAL. Mom, instead of talking about what you *don't* want, why not think about what you *do* want? What would that look like? *(Beat. Mary looks at her son.)*

Scene 7

Brian enters the house with a bag of food from Olive Garden. It's late, but Marty is hard at work on the folding table, making posters.

BRIAN. You're up? It's late.
MARTY. You shoulda heard them.
BRIAN. Heard who?
MARTY. At the meeting the other day. This meeting. Talking about what you get if you leave.
BRIAN. What do you get?
MARTY. And nobody, nobody talking about what you lose. The tragedy is so fresh. That's the problem, it's so fresh that nobody's thinking about what they'll lose.
BRIAN. *(Takes out the food.)* You want some Tour of Italy?
MARTY. *(Meh.)* Too much red sauce.
BRIAN. Eggplant?
MARTY. I never understood eggplant.
BRIAN. Seafood Alfredo?
MARTY. It's got shrimp?
BRIAN. *(Hoping this is the right answer.)* Yeah?
MARTY. Shrimp I'll take. *(Takes a container from Brian.)* Everyone's all excited, they got a plan. Apparently Rudy Tosetti's been doing research. He says they need everybody to be "united and organized."

That's the words he used. That means they gotta get eighty, ninety percent of the town on board, they want the government to even consider it. Eighty, ninety percent of people to sign these letters saying they'll never come back.
BRIAN. Never come back ...
MARTY. *(Emotional.)* Our whole community, just wiped out. Just ... gone. Can you even imagine?
BRIAN. Dad ...
MARTY. *(Pushing past it.)* That's a lot. A lot of people who might decide, might remember, why they're better off staying here. They think they're gonna be "united and organized"? I'm having a meeting of my own. I already got a petition started. *(Pushing a marker toward him.)* Grab a marker.
BRIAN. *(Hesitates.)* What're you gonna do, Dad, if you can't convince people to stay? If eighty percent of the town moves away, this place is gonna be a no man's land. You're gonna be living out here all alone, just you and Mom.
MARTY. It's not gonna happen.
BRIAN. But if it does? I don't agree with Sal. I think it's your life, your house, you do what you want ... but Emily told me Andrea and Phil are moving away —
MARTY. You saw Emily?
BRIAN. I mean Andrea and Phil? I'm just ... Look. You and me, we've always been the same. We get in our heads, this is the way it's gotta be. And it doesn't matter who gets hurt by it.
MARTY. So me wanting to stay in my house is the same as you breaking into somebody's SUV and ripping out their stereo system?
BRIAN. I'm not saying that.
MARTY. Selling it to that low-life you got arrested with —
BRIAN. Dad —
MARTY. Cheese Guy. What's his name?
BRIAN. That's not —
MARTY. Cheese Doodle?
BRIAN. Itz. Cheeze-Itz.
MARTY. Cheeze-Itz. Right. So dumb you were doing business with a guy named Cheeze-Itz.
BRIAN. I was doing a lot of dumb shit —
MARTY. In fact I think he named *himself* Cheeze-Itz, didn't he? Wasn't even a nickname.
BRIAN. Yeah.

MARTY. He named himself that. Right up there with Al Capone, this guy.
BRIAN. He thought it made him sound ...
MARTY. What? Pasteurized?
BRIAN. I don't know.
MARTY. I always wondered. The whole time, I wondered, this knucklehead was going around telling people to call him Cheeze-Itz. They musta had a name for you. *(Beat.)*
BRIAN. Camel Man.
MARTY. Camel Man.
BRIAN. Yeah, 'cause ... nevermind. It's stupid.
MARTY. I bet it is.
BRIAN. 'Cause I don't have to pee a lot. I can hold it for like a whole day. Sometimes two, if I eat lotsa salty pretzels and ... *(Catches his father's look.)* I told you it was stupid.
MARTY. At least it's fitting. Woulda been jarring, find out they were calling you Socrates or something like that. Einstein.
BRIAN. *(Cold.)* I guess taking stuff that's not mine just comes easy to me. Wonder where I learned that from. *(A tense beat. Brian exhales.)* Forget it. You wanna stay here, that's your right.
MARTY. You're damn right it is.
BRIAN. You wanna make Mom stay here, all alone, none of her friends nearby, that's your right too.
MARTY. I'm not making your mother do anything.
BRIAN. You sure about that? *(A cold beat.)*
MARTY. I'm surprised she still talks to you, Emily. After what you put her through.
BRIAN. We were young.
MARTY. Not that young.
BRIAN. It was her choice.
MARTY. You sure about that? *(Beat. Brian breaks a little. Marty softens.)* Hey, look. I shouldn'ta ... it's ancient history. You forget mine, I'll forget yours. *(Brian nods, an agreement. Silence.)*
BRIAN. You know I'm trying, Dad ... I'm really trying to stay on track.
MARTY. I know you are.
BRIAN. I was at a bar a couple weeks ago. I shouldn't have been there, but I was. This guy I know, this guy I met on the inside, he wanted to meet up.
MARTY. Aw Jesus, / Brian ...

BRIAN. / Everything he was saying, it was like he was offering me the sun, you know? Makin' it sound so easy.
MARTY. You got another chance here, Bri. Take it from me, you don't want to screw that up. Whatever you're feeling right now, whatever desperate thing you're feeling, it's a whole lot better than shame. 'Cause shame ... That's the thing makes you less than a man. *(Brian nods.)* What do you want, son? That's what you've got to ask yourself. What kind of life do you want?
BRIAN. I want ... I want the kind of life you've got.
MARTY. You can have it. 'Cause what did I ever do? I got married, had kids, worked my ass off in three grocery stores. You want a life like this, you can have it. But you gotta *fight* for it, kiddo. 'Cause if you don't fight for it, it's not worth anything. *(Beat. Brian takes a marker, posterboard.)*
BRIAN. So when's the meeting?
MARTY. Friday night. Make sure you get the date right. *(Brian nods, he starts writing. Sal enters.)* Look who's still here. There's eggplant, if that's your thing.
SAL. I'm allergic to eggplant.
BRIAN. You're allergic to eggplant?
SAL. Eggplant, tomatoes. I'm nightshade intolerant.
MARTY. *(Stares at Sal like he's speaking Swahili.)* What?
SAL. *(Clocks the marker in his brother's hand.)* What are you doing?
MARTY. Trying to save a community. You wouldn't know anything about it.
SAL. *(Takes out a crumpled poster from his pocket.)* That's what this is? This meeting you're having?
MARTY. Hey, where'd you get that?
SAL. Dunkin' Donuts. I did a coffee run for Nicky Gatto.
BRIAN. *("How's he doing?")* Nicky Gatto?
SAL. I was helping him clean out his attic. His brother-in-law almost died in the storm, and he's gotta see your posters telling him to "stand strong" —
MARTY. You better put it back.
SAL. I'm not putting it back!
MARTY. No problem. We got bigger ones now. *(To Brian.)* I'm gonna head up. Your shrimp's giving me heartburn.
BRIAN. Too spicy?
MARTY. No, it's good. You got your mother's talent for cooking. *(Kisses Brian on the head and shuffles off.)*

BRIAN. *(Pushes the pasta to Sal.)* Tell me that's not true.
SAL. *(Ignores it, livid.)* You're helping him with this?
BRIAN. They're talking about knocking down the whole place —
SAL. It *should* be knocked down! He's going around with his flyers and his petitions telling people to stand up for a community that *never shoulda been built here* to begin with.
BRIAN. I don't have too many good memories from the past ten years. Everything I've got that's worth remembering, it happened here.
SAL. So now you care about this place?
BRIAN. Yeah, maybe I do.
SAL. *(Sarcastic.)* This place has meaning for you? There's the house I got fucked up in. There's another house I got fucked up in.
BRIAN. Actually, yeah. It's a good reminder of how far I've come.
SAL. Great. As long as it's still all about you.
BRIAN. He lost everything. The stores, everybody who was working for him. He brought it on himself, I get that. But then the storm? It's like punching him when he's down. The house, this place, it's all he's got left. It's the one thing he can still control.
SAL. No, he can't. That's what he doesn't get. He's just a dog, barking at the wind. The two of you … you always got each other's back. Even when you were at your worst, stealing shit from little old ladies so you could get your pills and your H and all the other crap, he was still defending you.
BRIAN. He gave me plenty of talks.
SAL. Yeah. "Talks." Mom was falling to pieces. You were this close to killing yourself or somebody else and he was giving you "talks."
BRIAN. I thought you didn't want to "get into / this" —
SAL. / You know how bad it got? She was sick with it. I thought she was losing / her mind.
BRIAN. *I / know.*
SAL. / Every time the phone rang she jumped out of her skin. She was talking about you to strangers on the street: "My son's not doing well."
BRIAN. *(Sarcastic.)* So that's why you did it, for Mom?
SAL. Yeah, maybe I / did —
BRIAN. / When the cops came to you with that bullshit / story —
SAL. / I'm not the reason you got locked up, okay? Let's be clear on that.
BRIAN. Oh I'm clear. I had twenty-nine months to get "clear."
SAL. They *came* to me. To my *door*. What was I supposed to do?

BRIAN. I don't know. How 'bout *shut it*?
SAL. *(Laughs, bitter.)* I'm so tired of you and Dad always looking at me like I personally put you away.
BRIAN. If you hadn't told 'em where I was —
SAL. If you hadn't *been* there! You think what I did to you was so bad? What do you think it's like, watching your brother just ... *disintegrate*? What do you think it's like watching your kid brother just ... *(Beat.)* Dad wants to stay here. Mom wants to let him. You're *helping* him. Why do I even care? *Why do I even care? (He leaves.)*

Scene 8

A few days later. Andrea, Emily, and Mary sit at the table eating coffee cake, laughing.

MARY. *(To Emily.)* It's good to see you, honey. You look good.
EMILY. *(Waving it off, "I don't know.")* Eh.
ANDREA. She does look / good.
EMILY. / Mom ...
ANDREA. She lost weight.
MARY. I thought / so!
EMILY. / I gained weight.
ANDREA. Why would you tell people that?
MARY. It doesn't matter, you look good. You're gonna get back on that horse, no time.
EMILY. Actually, I'm enjoying being alone for a while.
MARY. Of course you are. *(Andrea shoots Emily a "bullshit" look.)*
EMILY. I *am*. It's peaceful. Clean. You never get home to find somebody left the dishes in the sink or finished watching *Game of Thrones* without you then *deleted* them all or ate the whole tub of hummus then put the empty container back in the fridge as if they didn't *notice* they'd finished it. They ate a whole thing of hummus without once even looking down into the container and seeing that it was empty? And then they just put it back so that you'd think there was still some left if you were counting on that for oh I don't know, maybe a little much-needed, much-deserved post-work

snack? Not to mention, who even eats a whole tub of hummus? That's a ridiculous amount of hummus. But now? If I purchase a tub of hummus, there's my hummus! Sitting there when I open the fridge, exactly as I left it. Completely full and waiting for me to enjoy. And I can have as much as I want because there is no else there. I am alone. I am utterly and completely alone. Except for my hummus. Just me and my hummus. *(Beat.)*
MARY. It's got a lot of fiber, hummus.
EMILY. I can't talk about this with the two of you. You both got married in the womb.
MARY. That doesn't mean we don't know what it is to be disappointed, or lonely. Sometimes the loneliest you can be is in a marriage, isn't it? *(Beat, a quasi-confession that takes Emily and Andrea aback.)*
ANDREA. Everything's okay, with you and Marty?
MARY. Oh yeah. I'm not talking about now. But over the course of thirty-some-odd years ... *(Changing the subject.)* This cake! It's so *moist*.
ANDREA. You should see my living room.
EMILY. *(Laughing.)* Mom ...
MARY. *(Laughs, takes Andrea's hand.)* I can't tell you how much I'll miss you. You and Phil both.
ANDREA. You could come with us, y'know. Montclair is very hip right now. And there's a community nearby, a 55-plus, it's not cheap, but it's got amenities. A pool. A clubhouse.
EMILY. Free denture fittings.
ANDREA. Very funny.
EMILY. Liver spot cleanings.
ANDREA. And you wonder why you're alone?
MARY. It's not for us.
ANDREA. Not for who? Not for Marty, maybe.
MARY. I can't very well move in without him, can I?
ANDREA. So you're thinking about it.
MARY. I'm not.
ANDREA. You're thinking about it. Mary Murphy, I've known you for thirty-four years. You're thinking about it. *(Mary doesn't reply.)* And if you're thinking about it, you should tell him so he can stop this ridiculous campaign he's on.
MARY. *(Taken aback.)* Ridiculous?
ANDREA. He's causing a lot of problems, Mary.
MARY. It's something he believes in. Nobody should be bullied into giving up their home.

ANDREA. Nobody should be bullied into keeping it either.
MARY. He's not bullying / anyone —
ANDREA. / Sweetheart, this is real money we're talking about. Money some of us need. Money you might need, you ever decide to tell him the truth and get out of here.
MARY. *(Sharp.)* Don't get involved in my marriage, Andrea. It's not your place.
ANDREA. I'm not getting involved in your marriage any more than your husband's getting involved in my finances.
EMILY. C'mon, you two. You're best friends.
ANDREA. And we'll stay best friends, forever, once we get out of here. *(Loaded.) If* we can get out of here. *(Then.)* He's a man of position, Marty. Despite everything.
EMILY. Mom —
MARY. Despite everything.
ANDREA. The Shriners. The volunteer fire department. These people listen to him.
MARY. That's what he's counting on. And don't you say "despite everything" to me. He's a good man.
EMILY. Of course / he is.
ANDREA. / No one's saying he's not.
MARY. Everybody messes up. It's human nature. He paid back every cent he owed. With his blood, sweat, and tears, he paid back what he owed.
ANDREA. I know that, Mary.
MARY. And it wasn't all his fault. The IRS was after him. It was entrapment.
ANDREA. It was a terrible thing, the whole ordeal. The important thing is you got to put it behind you and move on. Don't we all deserve that, the chance to move on? *(Mary breaks a little.)*
EMILY. Mary ...
MARY. I thought the storm was bad enough. All the destruction ... losing everything. That was enough heartache. But this. This turning on each other. It feels like we're at war with the whole town. *(Brian and Marty enter with a couple of their signs, hammers, etc. Mary wipes her eyes, tries to hide it. Andrea clocks the paraphernalia.)*
MARTY. Hey, it's a party! *(To Brian.)* We shoulda brought a piñata. *(Tension.)* What's going on?
MARY. *(Covering.)* Nothing. Cake. I'll get you a plate. *(She exits to the kitchen.)*

MARTY. Emily, get over here.
EMILY. Hi Marty. *(They hug. Brian and Emily exchange glances. Andrea notices.)*
ANDREA. Brian. It's good to see you.
BRIAN. You too, Andrea.
ANDREA. How was prison?
EMILY. Jesus, Mom. *(Mary reenters with plates.)*
MARTY. *(To Mary.)* So the insurance finally called?
MARY. They're gonna send someone as soon they can. There's a list, you know.
MARTY. I bet.
ANDREA. Phil's on his way, Marty. He wanted to talk to you. *(Mary looks at her.)*
BRIAN. *(To Emily.)* Did you, uh, did you want to see the deck? *(Awkward. Everyone stares.)*
EMILY. Sure. I'd love to "see the deck."
ANDREA. What's on the deck?
EMILY. Mom.
ANDREA. It's a deck.
MARTY. Not anymore.
ANDREA. You're gonna go make out.
EMILY. What?! Mom.
ANDREA. I'm not a fool, Emily.
EMILY. And I'm not a teenager.
ANDREA. That's right. You're a recent divorcée. It's even worse. You might as well be wearing a sign on your forehead that says, "Somebody, please, take advantage of me."
EMILY. *(To Brian.)* Let's go make out. *(Emily and Brian exit.)*
ANDREA. *(Calling.)* You better keep your hands where I can see them! Both of you!
MARY. Really, Andrea.
ANDREA. I'm sorry, sweetheart. But I think we all know that's not a good idea. *(Phil knocks on the "wall" and enters.)*
PHILIP. Is it just me, or is there a draft in here?
MARTY. Very funny. You want some cake?
PHILIP. No, I'm good.
MARTY. How 'bout a soda?
MARY. Why don't you see what he's doing here before you offer him the whole kitchen? *(A tense beat. Phil looks at Andrea.)*
ANDREA. What?

PHILIP. Christ, Andrea. If your mouth was any bigger you'd have to move it for street cleaning.
MARTY. What's going on?
MARY. They want you to stop the campaign. They were sent here. Like moles.
PHILIP. Mary, really —
ANDREA. Sent us here? Who do you think sent us?
MARY. I said you wouldn't. You care too much.
MARTY. That's exactly right.
PHILIP. Marty, listen, it's noble what you're doing. We all understand it, that it comes from a good place. But this petition you started, this crazy petition —
MARTY. *My* petition's crazy?
PHILIP. Micky Chrissmann said you told everyone at that meeting to start calling the press.
MARTY. And that meeting was just a start!
ANDREA. Just a start! Marty —
PHILIP. People start calling the press, there's no way we're getting that buy-out —
MARTY. That's the idea.
ANDREA. You're gonna ruin it for everyone!
MARTY. I'm not ruining it! I'm saving it!
PHILIP. Marty, *there's nothing left to save!* No one's saying you have to leave.
MARY. That's not true.
MARTY. No one's saying we have to leave? They get enough of you on board, they're gonna raze the whole place!
MARY. It just doesn't seem fair —
PHILIP. Of course it doesn't seem fair. There's nothing "fair" about it. But that's how it is! *(To Marty.)* You think, what, you can outsmart the next storm? You can make some kind of deal?
MARTY. I will not give up on this community.
PHILIP. "Community." You always had a screwed-up notion of what that was, you know that, Marty?
MARY. Watch yourself, Phil —
MARTY. I think I know what community is. I've been giving back to this community an awfully long time.
PHILIP. Right. Always giving back, giving back, but then you went out of your way to steal a few hundred thousand from the federal government.

MARY. Phil!
MARTY. I didn't steal anything. It was an accounting maneuver.
ANDREA. Marty, c'mon. Who do you think you're talking to?
MARTY. And I donated that   MARY. I can't take this. I can't.
money. Every cent I saved, I
donated right here in our backyard.
PHILIP. It wasn't yours to donate! You scammed the government for years, and now, ridiculous stupid miracle that it is, they may actually want to help you. They may actually want to GIVE you money and you won't take it! It's idiotic!
MARTY. You don't understand.
PHILIP. I don't understand. You're right, I don't.
MARTY. We can't go anywhere else.
PHILIP. Of course you can —
MARTY. WE CAN'T.
ANDREA. Why?!
MARTY. BECAUSE WE'RE BROKE. We're flat broke. *(Beat.)*
MARY. Marty …
PHILIP. That's why, if you sell the house —
MARTY. We can't sell it. We don't own it.
ANDREA. What do you mean you don't own it?
MARTY. I put it under Sal's name. So the Feds … *(Beat. Marty can't look at his wife.)*
PHILIP. So he'll get the money. He can give it to you.
MARTY. He won't.
ANDREA. Of course he will.
MARTY. I'm behind on the mortgage.
ANDREA. Mortgage?
MARTY. I borrowed against the house to put the money in the stores and then … He doesn't know he owns it.
PHILIP. Marty …
MARTY. At least here, I can work. People know me. They're willing to overlook the past. I go somewhere new? I'm a 62-year-old man with a history of fraud and tax evasion. I'm dirt. But here … They know me. They know me. *(Mary is overcome. She leaves the room.)*
ANDREA. Did she know all that? *(Beat.)* She's not happy here, Marty. She's being strong, toeing the line for you. That's what she's done her whole life. And she'll stay here, as long as you want her to, but I love that woman almost as much as you do, and I'm telling you: It's not what she wants. *(Marty looks away. Andrea exits to comfort Mary. Beat.)*

PHILIP. I can give you some money. Some more money.
MARTY. *(Shakes his head no.)* It's too much already. Knowing I'll never be able to pay you back … it kills me.
PHILIP. You gotta tell Sal he owns the place. He's gotta clear up the issue with the bank.
MARTY. I / know …
PHILIP. / Before it gets him in real trouble.
MARTY. I've been meaning to … but it always … And the truth is, the storm gave us some cover. What bank is gonna bother us about it now?
PHILIP. Marty.
MARTY. I'll come clean. Of course I'll come clean. But after some time. When I'm back on my feet. I was close, with the extra shifts at ShopRite. But then my back, the hotel … all those weeks at the hotel …
PHILIP. *(Swallows. This is hard for him.)* I'm sorry, Marty. But I can't let you do it.
MARTY. Can't let me do what?
PHILIP. I can't let you hold the whole town hostage 'cause you're in a terrible position. We're all struggling now. We all need some help right now.
MARTY. I'm trying to help.
PHILIP. Trying to help who?
MARTY. This is why I didn't want to tell you. I knew what you'd think: It's all about the money. It's not all about the money. You know I thought somebody else is gonna fight for this town. Somebody else is gonna stand up and I'm gonna join 'em. It won't be all my fight. But nobody else did. I hear 'em talking about it. People put everything they got into these houses. They don't want to go. But they're too afraid to say it.
PHILIP. Afraid of what?
MARTY. Afraid of the government.
PHILIP. Ah Jesus —
MARTY. Afraid of *you*. All of you, hellbent to get out of Dodge. To just Give Up. Some of us, we don't know how to do that, just Give Up. It's not in our blood. We hold on, come hell or high water. WE HOLD ON.
PHILIP. Because you're too scared to move on!
MARTY. YOU'RE WRONG! We're not scared. We're *terrified*. I. Am … *(Beat. Phil nods. It's a feeling he knows too, after all.)*

39

PHILIP. You gotta take down your posters. You gotta stop knocking on doors. And no talking to the press. You wanna stay here, that's your decision. But you gotta stop the crusade.
MARTY. Or what? I gotta stop the crusade, or what Phil?
PHILIP. Or I'm telling 'em, all of 'em ... about your situation. *(Beat.)*
MARTY. We've been friends for ...
PHILIP. A long time.
MARTY. We raised our kids together.
PHILIP. I know.
MARTY. We've been through heaven and hell. When Andrea caught you cheating? When you couldn't even show your face in church? Who helped you through that?
PHILIP. You stood by me. All the way.
MARTY. When Brian and Emily ...
PHILIP. It broke my heart. It was terrible, for all of us, but we moved on. And when the IRS closed your stores? Who was there for you? Who told the whole town it was just a trumped-up charge, even though I knew you'd been running that coupon scam for years. I knew. But things are different now. We're on our last legs. We don't have too many chances left to us. *(Beat.)* It wasn't supposed to be this hard, at 60. Now's when it was supposed to be easy. But it's not. And there's nothing I can do about that, for either of us, as much as I wish that I could. *(Silence.)* I'm not telling you to move. That's between you and your family. But I am telling you that everybody else is gonna leave. And you've got to let us. You've got to let us. *(He exits. Marty is alone, in the debris.)*

Scene 9

Brian and Emily, on the ruined deck. They share an electronic cigarette.

EMILY. It's not the same.
BRIAN. It's not s'posed to be.
EMILY. I kind of wish you didn't know that it was a fake. If you didn't know, you could maybe fool yourself ...

BRIAN. "There's no such thing as a little addiction." That's what they told us in therapy.
EMILY. Therapy huh?
BRIAN. And yoga too.
EMILY. Bullshit.
BRIAN. You wanna see my downward-facing dog? *(She laughs.)* I broke it off, with the girl at work.
EMILY. ... Okay.
BRIAN. We didn't have anything in common.
EMILY. That's probably a good thing, isn't it?
BRIAN. *(Dry.)* Thanks. *(Clears his throat: Here we go.)* Actually, being back here, it's really made me think a lot, about stuff, about what kinda life I want ...
EMILY. That's great. Thinking. Thinking's good.
BRIAN. And then, seeing you —
EMILY. I should go, there's still a lot to do —
BRIAN. Wait.
EMILY. — You wouldn't believe how many boxes —
BRIAN. Em.
EMILY. Turns out my parents are hoarders. We've got Ex-Lax that expired twenty years ago.
BRIAN. Em.
EMILY. I found a box of baby teeth from 1953.
BRIAN. Em. *(Takes her hand, silencing her.)* I know I don't deserve it, but I was hoping —
EMILY. No. *(Then.)* I get it, you thinking ... I mean I basically threw myself at you, talking about the beach and the past and my crappy divorce, but ... it was just for sex, okay? You and me, we always ... it was always good. Too good, obviously. And I've been a little ... *understaffed* lately. But that's all it was. I don't want you to think there's something here, some future here, that doesn't exist. I don't want you pinning your hopes on me.
BRIAN. It was just for sex.
EMILY. Yeah.
BRIAN. Well. That's flattering I guess.
EMILY. I just thought ... we both just got out of prison, in our own way. So.
BRIAN. Yeah. *(Beat, a joke.)* At least you got to cut your own toenails. *(Emily laughs.)* And some visitors now and then.
EMILY. You got visitors. Your mother — ?

BRIAN. Yeah, sure. My parents.
EMILY. Sal?
BRIAN. Nah. Too much bad blood.
EMILY. It wasn't easy for him to do what he did. He thought he was helping you.
BRIAN. Yeah.
EMILY. He did. You know him and your father didn't speak for over a year. It was Christmas before they could even be in the same room together. *(This is news to Brian.)*
BRIAN. You know Dad. Never back off. No matter what.
EMILY. *(Trying to cheer him up.)* Remember the night we snuck in your dad's store and ate every flavor of Häagen Dazs and he caught us? Y'know what he did, after he was done yelling at you? *(Brian shakes his head no.)* He gave me a wink and a pint of Rocky Road. *(They laugh.)*
BRIAN. He loved making people happy. It made him feel important. *(Beat.)* I'd like to make someone happy. Not even a lot of people. Just one person.
EMILY. It's a good goal.
BRIAN. I mean it. *(He looks her in the eye.)*
EMILY. Brian ...
BRIAN. You gotta give me a shot. You and me, we're like bumper cars. Our whole lives, smashing into each other, running away, smashing into each other again and again ...
EMILY. "There's no such thing as a little addiction."
BRIAN. It's not addiction. It's love.
EMILY. Come on ...
BRIAN. What else could it be? You think I wanted to come back here? To help? I wanted to run away as far as I could. But Sal told me for once I should do something for somebody else, and what do I find when I get here? You, in your big hat and your dad's coat, looking like a homeless person —
EMILY. I didn't look homeless.
BRIAN. You didn't look *not* homeless. But it didn't matter, 'cause the minute I saw you ... *(She looks at him, hard.)*
EMILY. I'm not as strong as I was back then.
BRIAN. And I'm not as stupid. At least, I hope not.
EMILY. You were never stupid.
BRIAN. You were always the only one who thought that. *(Beat. He pulls her close to him. Emily takes a deep breath.)*
EMILY. My mother's gonna kill me. *(Brian smiles. He kisses her.)*

42

Scene 10

Later that day. Classic pop, like the Beach Boys, on the radio.* Marty working.

Mary enters silently in her coat, with a grocery bag and her car keys. She watches her husband for a moment, her face drawn. Finally, she turns off the radio. Marty looks up, startled.

MARTY. Mare. What're you doing, you scared me ...
MARY. *(A little strange; far away.)* I went shopping. I was about to buy some coffee when I remembered we don't have a machine. Flew off the counter in the storm. It was the first thing I threw out.
MARTY. We'll get a new one. Add it to the list.
MARY. The list. *(Pause. She continues to stare at him, hard, unyielding.)*
MARTY. Listen —
MARY. No.
MARTY. Mare —
MARY. No. I've been listening to you for thirty-eight years. Listening and listening and listening. When you wanted to move to this house, I listened. When you wanted to buy that first store even though we had no money to do it, I listened. Two kids, not three, though I wanted that third one so badly ... When times were hard and you couldn't make do, I started working at the library. That was listening too. Listening to what you couldn't say. After all these years of listening you'd think I was pretty good at it. You'd think I'd remember if I heard you say, heard you *mention*, that you'd been undermining your own son.
MARTY. Mary —
MARY. *(Fierce.)* Your own son. MY SON. And for what? To keep this house? LOOK AROUND. Look at what you wanted so badly you were willing to throw away Sal's entire future!
MARTY. I was gonna —
MARY. BULLSHIT.
MARTY. *(Taken aback by the curse.)* Mary.

* See Special Note on Songs and Recordings on copyright page.

MARY. What I can't say bullshit? Because Mary doesn't curse? Well *Mary's cursing now*. It's BULLSHIT. ALL BULLSHIT. Trust me, God will understand. He gets lied to all the time. *(Marty reaches for her but she shakes him off.)*
MARTY. You gotta let me —
MARY. I don't want to hear it.
MARTY. *(Desperate.)* You gotta let me, you gotta … I felt so … Let them take this house? This house my own father gave me? And I was gonna tell him, but then the stuff with Brian, what / he did to Brian —
MARY. / We're not talking about that. I told you I'm never talking about that again!
MARTY. So I was angry! And I was wrong.
MARY. Yes you were. About a few things. Not least of which was thinking that I'd want to stay in this house if it meant hurting my own children.
MARTY. I'm gonna make it right —
MARY. You can't make it right.
MARTY. Mary. Please. I'm gonna fix it. All of it.
MARY. Yeah? *Put it on the list. (A terrible beat.)* I called Sally. He's on his way.
MARTY. *(Looks at her, stricken.)* You told him — ?
MARY. No. That's for you to do. And you're gonna do it Marty. You're gonna do it, or you can stay here in this, this *nothing*, all by yourself. 'Cause I'm leaving. I will leave you.
MARTY. Don't talk like that.
MARY. You don't think I'll do it? Look around you. Everyone we know is moving on. Giving up everything they've known their whole lives. Hearts are broken all over this place. What's one more? What's one more destroyed thing? Honestly, who would even notice?
MARTY. *(Very small.)* Mare, please …
MARY. It's not that I thought you were always right all these years. I'm not that stupid. I didn't think you were right. I thought you were *good. (Beat. Sal enters. He immediately picks up on the strange tension.)*
SAL. Hello? Mom? What's going on?
MARY. *(To Marty.)* Y'know where we went, Sal and I? To the real estate office. *(Marty looks at her, wounded.)* But I couldn't stay. I didn't want to *hurt you. (She exits to the kitchen.)*
SAL. What's going on? *(At a complete loss for what to do, Marty starts working on the hole in the wall.)*

MARTY. I gotta get this sheetrock up.
SAL. That's why I left work early? Watch you hang sheetrock?
MARTY. You know why I'm so intent on fixing this house? All the hard work, y'know who that's for? YOU. You and your brother. My dad gave me this house and I wanted to give it to you. That's always been the plan.
SAL. I don't want the house, Dad.
MARTY. Now. Sure. But you don't know. Things change. You might need more room. Or maybe you'll just use it as a bungalow. The point is, you should have it. A father should be able to leave his son something.
SAL. Dad. Why did Mom tell me to get over here?
MARTY. I want you to know what was in my head. It wasn't just about your mother, though I was worried about her too —
SAL. What was in your head / when?
MARTY. / I provide for her. I know it's not very modern, but it's what we do —
SAL. DAD. What did you do? *(Beat.)*
MARTY. The house. I put the house ... I gave you the house. As a gift. *(Beat.)*
SAL. A "gift."
MARTY. So the Feds ...
SAL. You "gave" me the house. You put the house in my name without telling me.
MARTY. I didn't want to burden you.
SAL. *(A crazy laugh.)* You didn't want to — ?! How do you even do that?!
MARTY. There's ways.
SAL. There's ways. And the IRS didn't notice?
MARTY. *(Re: Jesus.)* I guess somebody's looking out for me.
SAL. No Dad, that's not how it works. Jesus doesn't "look out" for tax evaders.
MARTY. He looks out for this one. *(Beat.)*
SAL. So I own this house.
MARTY. *(Small.)* You own part of it.
SAL. Who owns the rest?
MARTY. *(Almost impossible to say.)* I'm behind. On the mortgage. *(A terrible pause.)*
SAL. You're fucking kidding me.
MARTY. It's just a couple payments —

SAL. *Are you fucking kidding me?* What's a "couple"? What's a "couple" Dad?
MARTY. Three months.
SAL. Three months.
MARTY. Four, if you count December ...
SAL. It's January. *(Marty shrugs. Sal is completely overwhelmed.)* Were you gonna tell me, or just wait for the bank to figure it out and take me to court?
MARTY. I was gonna tell you, when we were solvent I was gonna tell you.
SAL. You know what this does to me? To my marriage? Jenn's trying to start a business! Next week she's gonna walk into the bank and they're gonna tell her, what? Sorry, your credit score's basically zero?
MARTY. They won't do that.
SAL. *What planet do you live on?* Something like this gets on your credit report, you can't get money for years! You can't get a new job, a new place to live — what if we were gonna move? You think a landlord's gonna approve us with something like this on our record?
MARTY. *(Small.)* I didn't think about that.
SAL. Clearly. And you also *clearly* didn't think I'd help.
MARTY. You know. Family's never been your first concern.
SAL. *(Bitter laugh.)* Yeah I know. That's the old line. "Sal's too good for his family. That's why he moved away. That's why he snitched on his own brother."
MARTY. If the shoe fits.
SAL. You know I've been sending Mom money?
MARTY. *(Surprised.)* What are you talking about?
SAL. Not just a little here or there. A pretty good amount of money. At first, Jenn was supportive. "Your parents are in need, we've got to help them." She really meant it, too. But then months turned to years. I couldn't just stop sending it. Of course, Mom doesn't know Jenn knows. And every time we see you guys Mom *needles* her about some stupid thing, asthma rates in the city or how much take-out we eat or ... which doesn't really *help* ... It's almost destroyed my marriage. And now this ...
MARTY. I didn't ask you to send money.
SAL. No, you just put your house in my name and hoped I wouldn't find out. You couldn't ask for help. You had to take it. As if it was due to you. Which just about sums you up, doesn't it Dad?
MARTY. We'll give you the money back.

SAL. How? You've got some investments I don't know about? Some internet startup or something?
MARTY. I'm still working. I can still work.
SAL. You're 62 years old.
MARTY. I CAN STILL WORK.
SAL. For how long? Another five, ten years? For what, sixteen bucks an hour? How're you paying me back Dad?
MARTY. *(Smaller.)* I can still work.
SAL. It's OVER. When are you gonna see that? When are you gonna stop with all the stupid scams, stop PRETENDING you've got a life YOU DON'T HAVE. Y'know why you want to "save this community"? Why you're so obsessed with it? It's not 'cause you love these people so much. It's cause *they* loved *you*. You lied to them your whole life and they still loved you and you know no one else on Earth is gonna be that STUPID. *(Brian enters.)*
BRIAN. What's going on? I heard screaming —
SAL. *(To Marty.)* Tell him. TELL HIM.
MARTY. I'm behind on the house. *(Beat.)* It's in Sal's name and ... *(Beat. Marty can't look at his sons.)*
BRIAN. Jesus Dad ...
MARTY. *(To Sal.)* I just wanted you to have it, I wanted —
SAL. I DON'T WANT IT. I don't want the house. I don't want the money. Just ... some recognition. Or ... forgiveness for doing *the right thing*. I'd just like to feel, for once I'd like to feel like I actually *belong* here.
MARTY. *(Looks at him.)* I thought you said none of us belonged here anymore.
SAL. You don't.
MARTY. Well it's up to you now, isn't it? It's your house.
SAL. Yeah, I guess it is.
MARTY. I'm ... I'm uh ... *(Another terrible beat. Marty pushes past Brian for the door.)*
BRIAN. Dad ... *(Marty exits. Brian looks at Sal. A moment. Brian follows after Marty, leaving Sal alone.)*

Scene 11

Hours later. Night. Sal is alone in his childhood home. Mary enters the room in her housecoat, surprised to see him.

MARY. You're still here?
SAL. Jenn didn't want me to come home.
MARY. Oh Sally. I'm so / sorry.
SAL. / It's fine.
MARY. It's not fine. I've been taking your money all this time ... Trying to protect him, his "dignity." I was so busy trying to protect him, I forgot about you.
SAL. You didn't forget about me. *(Mary looks at away, ashamed. He goes to her.)* Mom. Ask me what the key to life is. *(Mary looks at her son, grateful. A moment between them. Marty enters, lugging his dug-up signs, which he drops by the door. He and Sal exchange a look.)* Where's Brian?
MARTY. Getting the last of them.
SAL. Guess the campaign's over? *(A cold beat.)*
MARTY. I'm gonna go pack.
SAL. Dad —
MARTY. *(To Mary.)* You should start too.
MARY. Don't tell me what I should do.
SAL. Dad —
MARTY. She doesn't pack fast. We once missed a cruise cause she was still packing.
MARY. 'Cause I was packing for *you*! *I was always packing for you!*
SAL. I'm not making you move. *(Beat.)* I'm not making you move. *(Silence.)* I called the bank. I'll pay what you owe, but you're gonna have to work out some loan modification going forward. I can give you enough for the next few months, but after that ...
MARY. Sally.
SAL. It's gonna push back Jenn's plans but, if we dig into our savings ...
MARY. We can't ask you to do that ...
SAL. *(Strong.)* And you're gonna put it back in your name. Immediately. *(Beat. Marty nods.)* Jenn's mad. Furious.
MARY. She has every right to be.

SAL. But she also, somehow ... *(Beat.)*
MARTY. Why?
SAL. Because it's your house. It should be your choice. But it has to be hers, too. You've lived your whole life here. And you never wanted to leave. It's not something I understand, but ... I wish I did. *(Marty and Mary are speechless. Sal heads to the door.)*
MARTY. You know why I put this place in your name? *(Sal stops.)* Because I *could*. You worked your ass off. You did it yourself, the right way. God knows you didn't learn that from me. I've made a lot of mistakes in my life. I've made a lot of mistakes. But I'll do better ... *(To Mary.)* I'll be better ... *(A heavy silence.)*
SAL. Are you two gonna be okay? *(Marty and Mary look at each other. It's a question too hard to answer. She exits. Marty is deeply wounded.)* Dad ...
MARTY. Letting us stay here ... It's very generous of you.
SAL. Yeah well, I'm a generous guy. I guess that's something you didn't know about me.
MARTY. I know more than you think.
SAL. Yeah? *(Beat.)*
MARTY. I know ... I know it took courage to do what you did, saving Brian from himself. It still makes me ... But always I knew, it took great courage.
SAL. I wish you coulda told me that. I really wish you woulda told me that.
MARTY. You gotta tell Jenn ... how sorry I am ...
SAL. I will. Eventually.
MARTY. She's gotta know ... how much it means to me ...
SAL. I can't really tell her anything right / now.
MARTY. / She's gotta know ... *(To Sal.)* how grateful I am.
SAL. *(Accepts it, then —)* If she ever picks up the phone I'll — *(Marty grabs his son. It surprises Sal. Maybe it surprises them both. They stand for a moment in the embrace, then Marty pulls away gently, awkwardly. Beat.)*
MARTY. I've been wanting to tell you for a while, about the house. But how do you tell somebody you did something ... how do you tell somebody you love ... *(Sal looks at Marty. It means a lot. It means everything.)*

Scene 12

A week or so later. Sal, Brian, Marty, and Mary eat dinner around the card table. There's a tablecloth. It looks almost like home.

BRIAN. So you're giving up the half-bedroom.
SAL. Jenn needs a place to work and it's really not a half ... it's really just a closet without a door. We can save some money and get a two-bedroom if we go to Brooklyn.
MARTY. Brooklyn.
SAL. Dad. Don't start.
BRIAN. Tell her to come over to my place. Twenty guys share the bathroom and the couch has bedbugs, but it's a great place to start a PR firm.
SAL. Thanks, I'll tell her.   MARTY. That's an idea.
MARTY. We'll come out and help you move.
SAL. That's okay, Dad. We're gonna hire someone.
MARY. You're gonna need some new furniture. We could go shopping. *(Taking out her phone.)* I'll call Jenn —
SAL. Mom. I really don't think she wants to hear from you guys right now. *(A small, sad beat. Mary puts away the phone. Desperate to change the subject.)* Looks like they're gonna get their buy-out. Front page.
MARTY. The whole town's packing up. Even Jerry.
BRIAN. Jerry. Where the hell is Jerry going?
MARY. His ex-wife's taking him in.
SAL. Didn't he sleep with her sister?
MARY. *(With a shrug.)* Yeah, but she's dead now, the sister. And her other sister lives in Norway, so I guess she figures it's safe.
MARTY. They'll all regret it. When summer comes and they're living fifty miles from the nearest beach. Once you've lived by the water, it gets in your soul.
MARY. And your carpeting.
MARTY. You've been talking to Andrea too much.
MARY. They finished up yesterday. Gone forever.
BRIAN. They're not dead. They moved to Montclair.

50

SAL. *(To Marty.)* Did you talk to them, before they left?
MARTY. *(A "no.")* We'll see them.
SAL. That's good. Hold a grudge. That's a productive way to spend the last twenty years of your life.
MARTY. Friends aren't blood.
BRIAN. They are if I marry Emily. *(Beat. Everyone stares at Brian.)* We're thinking of getting a place together.
MARY. I guess it's good they moved. They're never talking to us again anyway.
MARTY. Isn't this a little fast?
BRIAN. We've known each other our whole lives.
MARY. But you're just now getting back on your feet, and she's —
BRIAN. Mom. It's the right thing. I can tell. I know it is. And the rents here are nothing now. We could get a really good-size place.
SAL. Here? You're gonna move back?
BRIAN. *(With a shrug.)* Not *right* here but ... it's home.
MARY. *(Moving on.)* Does anyone want more? *(Sal and Brian exchange a look, then —)*
BRIAN and SAL. Yeah, sure, delicious, so good ... *(Mary shovels more on their plates.)*
MARY. Who knew you could make a whole chicken in the microwave?
MARTY. Another gourmet meal. *(He takes Mary's hand and kisses it. She pulls away. Sal and Brian notice. Marty is quietly devastated. Mary stands and takes the plates.)*
MARY. *(Pained, an excuse.)* I've gotta get ... something, in the kitchen ... *(Exits.)*
MARTY. It'll be okay. Once everything's back to normal.
SAL. I don't think there is a back to normal, Dad.
MARTY. *(Nods. He looks at his sons.)* I hate this storm. I hate everything about it. But to sit here, in my house, with the two of you ... *(Takes their hands. A moment, then he gets up and brings some cups into the kitchen, leaving Sal and Brian alone.)*
BRIAN. You gonna be okay, you and Jenn?
SAL. *(Shakes his head, unsure.)* She's been working non-stop, crazy hours. It's been everything. She was about to sign a lease. Picking up that phone I thought ... *(Shakes his head.)* And then she just ... Tells me to give them the money. Whatever they need. She's nothing like Mom. But in some ways ...
BRIAN. In some ways she's pretty awesome.
SAL. I really don't deserve her.

BRIAN. Yeah you do. *(Beat.)* You know I never really thanked you, for what you did. Mostly 'cause I fucking hated you, so a thank-you never really felt appropriate, but ... *(Sal nods, takes it in. They sit for a moment in silence.)* So.
SAL. So.
BRIAN. You're not gonna miss it? This town? All the people we grew up with?
SAL. Yeah I'm gonna miss it. I already do.

Scene 13

Very early morning. The sun is just beginning to climb into the sky. Mary is bundled, sitting awake at the card table, an empty mug in front of her. Marty enters in his pajamas and robe.

MARTY. I got up to go to the bathroom. You weren't there.
MARY. I couldn't sleep. Thought I'd greet the sun.
MARTY. What's in the mug?
MARY. Nothing. I just missed the feeling of holding a mug in the early morning. *(Marty nods. He goes into the kitchen and returns with his own empty mug. Mary smiles.)*
MARTY. We could walk out to the beach for sunrise. Like we used to.
MARY. No. *(Marty looks at her, sad.)*
MARTY. You think ... you think you could ever forgive me?
MARY. I don't know. I just don't know. *(Beat.)*
MARTY. I found the paperwork. *(Mary looks up, surprised.)* The buy-out application. I was looking for a pair of scissors ...
MARY. Andrea brought it. I should've told you.
MARTY. Andrea filled it out, too? *(Silence.)*
MARY. We're gonna be grandparents.
MARTY. *(Surprised.)* What?
MARY. Eventually. *(Marty laughs.)* I'm worried, if we stay, they'll never feel comfortable, they'll be afraid ... That's not it. I'll always be afraid. *(Pause.)*

MARTY. I had a feeling you'd say that. *(He takes out an envelope.)* It's got a stamp and everything. All you gotta do is put it in the mailbox. *(A gentle joke.)* If you can find one that's still standing. *(Mary looks at the envelope, then at him, appreciatively. She takes it.)* Hopefully, the appraiser'll see it for what it's worth. What it was.
MARY. Marty.
MARTY. I had it in my head, lodged in my head, I kept thinking: I gotta keep this house. How can I lose this house? Turns out, there's really only one thing I can't lose. *(Mary takes his hand. Beat. Trying.)* We don't have to stay here you know, on the Island. We could go anywhere we wanted.
MARY. Like where?
MARTY. I don't know. Paris.
MARY. Paris!
MARTY. Tokyo.
MARY. *(Laughs.)* Mexico.
MARTY. Mexico! Bake in the sun all day.
MARY. Drink margaritas for breakfast.
MARTY. Get ourselves a little place by the water … *(Beat.)*
MARY. Let's go for a walk.
MARTY. The beach? *(Mary nods. Marty goes to the door and holds it open for his wife. Mary stands and takes the envelope. She joins her husband at the door. Marty puts his arm around Mary. They pause to take in the house. Marty kisses Mary on the forehead and they head off into the cold.)*

End of Play

PROPERTY LIST

Surgical masks
Magic Bullet blender
Plastic gloves
Cell phone
Contractor bags
Suitcases with home decor, such as a cross and a framed photo or embroidered saying
Six-pack of beer
Bag of hardware
Bag of food from Olive Garden
Posters and poster making supplies
Coffee cake
Signs, hammers, etc.
Electronic cigarette
Radio
Grocery bag
Car keys
Plates of dinner
Mugs
Envelope with a stamp